SOUPS & SANDWICHES

TORMONT

© J.B. Fairfax Press Pty Limited

ALL RIGHTS RESERVED. No part of this book may be reproduced or transmitted in any form or by any means, electronic or mechanical, including photocopying, recording, or by any information storage and retrieval system, without permission in writing from the publisher.

Graphic Design: Zapp

This edition published in 1996 by:
Tormont Publications Inc.
338 Saint Antoine St. East
Montreal, Canada H2Y 1A3
Tel. (514) 954-1441
Fax (514) 954-5086

ISBN 2-7641-0104-X
Printed in Canada

Contents

30-Minute Soups   4

Hearty Main Course Soups   14

Vegetarian Soups   36

Cool Summer Soups   50

Stocks   60

Soup Garnishes   61

Sandwiches and Snacks   62

Table of Measures   79

Index   80

30-Minute Soups

All too many modern cooks overlook the pleasures of homemade soups, under the mistaken impression that a good soup requires hours of chopping and simmering.

But if you keep a few simple ingredients on hand, and make use of modern conveniences such as a blender or food processor, you can turn out delicious soups of your own in less than 30 minutes, and for a fraction of the price of ready-made versions.

In this chapter you will find quick soup solutions for every occasion, whether you crave a cool summer concoction that involves no cooking at all, or a substantial meal-in-a-bowl that will satisfy the heartiest appetites.

Avocado Summer Soup, Chilled Melon and Cucumber Soup (page 6)

Chilled Melon and Cucumber Soup

1	cantaloupe melon, peeled and seeded	1
4	cucumbers, peeled and seeded	4
2 tbsp	honey	30 mL
2 tbsp	lemon juice	30 mL
8-12	mint sprigs	8-12

♦ ◆ ♦

1. In a food processor or blender, purée melon and cucumbers until smooth; strain. Add honey and lemon juice; pour mixture into a bowl, cover and set aside.

2. Roughly chop mint (reserving some for garnish) and stir into puréed mixture. Let mixture stand for about 5 hours at room temperature.

3. Remove chopped mint from soup, and chill until ready to serve.

Serves 6

Avocado Summer Soup

4	ripe avocados, peeled and pitted	4
2 cups	chicken stock	500 mL
1/2 cup	dry white wine	125 mL
1/4 cup	whipping cream	60 mL
3 tbsp	lemon juice	45 mL
	red bell pepper strips and dill sprigs for garnish	

♦ ◆ ♦

1. Chop avocado flesh and purée in food processor or blender.

2. While motor is running add stock, wine, cream, and lemon juice, blend until smooth.

3. Chill soup until ready to serve. Garnish with red pepper and dill sprigs.

Serves 6

Chilled Spinach Soup with Sour Cream

1	onion, chopped	1
4 tbsp	unsalted butter	60 mL
1 tbsp	all-purpose flour	15 mL
2 1/2 cups	chicken stock	625 mL
1 lb	fresh spinach, rinsed, cooked and chopped	450 g
1 3/4 cups	sour cream	425 mL
	salt and freshly ground black pepper	

♦ ◆ ♦

1. Cook onion in butter over medium heat until soft, about 5 minutes. Add flour and cook for 2 minutes, stirring constantly.

2. Gradually add stock, stirring constantly. Cook until mixture thickens. Add spinach, season to taste with salt and pepper, and cook for 5 minutes. Purée in a food processor or blender. Add 1 1/4 cups (310 mL) sour cream and blend well.

3. Pour into a serving dish, allow to cool, cover and refrigerate for at least 4 hours or overnight.

4. When ready to serve correct seasoning, ladle soup into bowls and swirl in remaining sour cream.

Serves 6

TIP: *A thawed package of frozen chopped spinach can be substituted for the fresh spinach.*

Cream of Summer Squash Soup

1 tbsp	butter	15 mL
1 lb	yellow summer squash or zucchini, chopped	450 g
1	onion, chopped	1
2 cups	chicken stock	500 mL
1 cup	sour cream	250 mL
	pinch nutmeg	
	salt and freshly ground black pepper	
	sour cream and chopped chives for garnish	

♦ ♦

1. Melt butter in a large saucepan, add squash and onion, and cook over medium-high heat until squash is tender. Add stock to mixture, bring to a boil and simmer for 20 minutes, or until squash falls apart.

2. Remove from heat and purée until smooth. Transfer mixture to a clean saucepan, mix in cream and nutmeg, and season to taste. Reheat, garnish and serve.

Serves 4

TIP: *Very hot liquids may crack some blender or food processor bowls, or may cause splattering. Check manufacturer's instructions for your appliance to determine whether you should allow hot liquids to cool somewhat before processing.*

Chilled Coriander and Yogurt Soup

2 ½ cups	plain yogurt	625 mL
1 ½ cups	packed, chopped fresh coriander, leaves and tender stems only	375 mL
½	onion, finely chopped	½
1 cup	light cream	250 mL
3 cups	chicken stock	750 mL
	parsley sprig for garnish	

1. In a food processor or blender, purée yogurt, coriander, onion and cream until smooth.
2. Pour into a large container, add stock, and mix well.
3. Cover and chill until ready to serve. Garnish with parsley or fresh coriander.

Serves 6

Cream of Corn and Red Pepper Soup

2	red bell peppers	2
2 tsp	arrowroot	10 mL
2	onions, chopped	2
2 cups	chicken stock	500 mL
2 cups	corn kernels, fresh or frozen	500 mL
1 cup	light cream	250 mL
	chopped chives for garnish	

1. Roast red peppers under a preheated broiler until charred, about 5 minutes. Seal in a paper bag for 10 minutes. Remove skin, seeds and stems. Purée flesh in a blender until smooth; strain.
2. Combine arrowroot with 3 tbsp (45 mL) of red pepper purée, mix to a paste. Heat remaining purée in small saucepan until boiling, stir in arrowroot paste until mixture thickens, then remove from heat.
3. In a large saucepan combine onions and stock, and cook for 5 minutes. Add corn and cook 10 minutes. Purée soup in food processor or blender, then return to saucepan. Reheat without boiling. Add cream. Serve soup hot and garnish each portion with a swirl of red pepper purée and a few chives.

Serves 4

Watercress Soup with Orange

3 cups	chicken stock	750 mL
1	large potato, peeled and chopped	1
2 cups	fresh watercress, leaves and tender stems only	500 mL
¾ cup	light cream	185 mL
1 cup	unsweetened orange juice	250 mL
	watercress sprigs for garnish	

1. Bring chicken stock to a boil, add potato and cook until tender. Add watercress, cover and cook 3 minutes.
2. Place mixture into a blender or food processor and blend for 2 minutes. Add cream and orange juice, then blend for 2-3 seconds. Return to saucepan and slowly reheat, being careful not to boil. Serve soup hot, garnished with sprigs of watercress if desired.

Serves 6

Chilled Coriander and Yogurt Soup, Cream of Corn and Red Pepper Soup

Yogurt Soup

6 cups	chicken stock	1.5 L
1/3 cup	long-grain rice	85 mL
2 1/2 cups	plain low-fat yogurt	625 mL
3	egg yolks	3
2 tbsp	butter, melted	30 mL
2 tbsp	chopped fresh mint	30 mL

1. Bring chicken stock to a boil in a large saucepan. Add rice and cook for 15 minutes or until rice is tender.

2. In a second large saucepan, beat yogurt and egg yolks together until well mixed.

3. Slowly pour hot stock and rice mixture into pan containing yogurt and egg yolks. Heat gently, stirring constantly, until soup thickens.

4. Ladle soup into serving bowls. Spoon a little melted butter onto each portion and sprinkle with mint. Serve at once.

Serves 4

Macaroni and Vegetable Soup

6 cups	chicken stock	1.5 L
1 1/2 tbsp	tomato paste	25 mL
2	carrots, chopped	2
1	onion, chopped	1
1	small green bell pepper, chopped	1
2 tsp	bottled green peppercorns, crushed	10 mL
1 tbsp	chopped fresh basil	15 mL
4 oz	short tube pasta or elbow macaroni	120 g

1. Bring stock and tomato paste to a boil, add carrots, onion, green pepper, peppercorns and basil, and cook for 10 minutes.

2. Add macaroni, cook for 10 minutes or until macaroni is *al dente* and vegetables are tender. Serve immediately.

Serves 4

Italian Fettuccine Consommé

3	garlic cloves, crushed	3
½ cup	chopped canned tomatoes	125 mL
1 cup	chicken stock	250 mL
¾ lb	fettuccine	350 g
2 tbsp	chopped fresh basil	30 mL
1 ¼ cups	grated Parmesan cheese	310 mL
	basil sprigs for garnish	

♦ ♦ ♦

1. Place 3 tbsp (45 mL) water in a large saucepan over medium heat; add garlic and 'sweat' until water has evaporated.

2. Add tomatoes, 3 cups (750 mL) water and chicken stock and bring to a boil. Add fettuccine and cook until *al dente*.

3. Remove from heat, stir in chopped basil and half the cheese. Garnish each serving with a basil sprig and remaining cheese.

Serves 6

TIP: Stir in some leftover cooked broccoli, a few peas or anything else that strikes your fancy to add color and nutrition.

Beggar's Soup

1	loaf French bread, cut into thin slices	1
1	garlic clove, halved	1
4 cups	chicken stock	1 L
2-3 cups	broccoli florets	500-750 mL
2/3 cup	freshly grated Parmesan cheese	165 mL

♦ ♦ ♦

1. Toast bread on both sides. Rub cut side of the garlic generously over each slice of toast.

2. Bring chicken stock to a boil in a large saucepan. Add broccoli and cook for 30 seconds until broccoli is tender-crisp.

3. Ladle soup into heated soup bowls, place two or three slices of garlic toast in each, and sprinkle with Parmesan.

Serves 4

Variation

Use thinly sliced mushrooms instead of broccoli and substitute garlic croutons — bread cubes cooked in garlic butter until crisp — for the garlic toast. If you feel extravagant, brown the mushrooms lightly in butter before adding to the stock.

HEARTY MAIN COURSE SOUPS

Comfort in a cup or bowl — that's the simple secret of a hearty hot soup, especially in the winter.

Plan your meal around a robust noodle soup with meatballs, or a creamy bisque of artichokes and shrimp, and the rest of the meal is a snap. A salad and some bread is all you need, followed by some fresh fruit or cookies.

Noodle Soup with Basil and Meatballs, Pea and Ham Soup (page 16)

Noodle Soup with Basil and Meatballs

1/2 lb	ground chicken	225 g
1	egg, lightly beaten	1
1/3 cup	dried breadcrumbs	85 mL
2 tbsp	finely grated Parmesan cheese	30 mL
1 tbsp	finely chopped fresh basil	15 mL
1 tbsp	tomato paste	15 mL
3	garlic cloves, crushed	3
1	onion, very finely chopped	1
1 tbsp	olive oil	15 mL
2	carrots, cut into thin strips	2
4 cups	chicken stock	1 L
1/4 lb	vermicelli noodles	110 g
1 tsp	crushed black peppercorns	5 mL
	fresh basil for garnish	

1. Combine ground chicken, egg, breadcrumbs, Parmesan cheese, basil, tomato paste, garlic and onion in a medium bowl, and mix well. Form mixture into about 18 meatballs, 3/4 inch (2 cm) in diameter; set aside.

2. Heat oil in a large, nonstick skillet, add meatballs and brown over medium heat. Continue to cook until meatballs are cooked through, about 6 minutes. Add carrots to skillet and cook 3 minutes.

3. Bring stock to a boil in a large saucepan, add pasta and cook until *al dente*. Stir in carrots and meatballs. Garnish with crushed peppercorns and basil, and serve.

Serves 4

Pea and Ham Soup

2 tbsp	olive oil	30 mL
2 tbsp	butter	30 mL
1/4 lb	cooked ham, diced	110 g
2	garlic cloves, crushed	2
1	onion, finely chopped	1
1/4 lb	mushrooms, sliced	110 g
4 cups	chicken stock	1 L
1/2 tsp	crushed black peppercorns	2 mL
1/2 tsp	paprika	2 mL
3	celery stalks, finely chopped	3
1 cup	packed shredded lettuce	250 mL
1 1/2 cups	green peas, fresh or frozen	375 mL
1 oz	ditalini or other tiny pasta	28 g
2 tbsp	finely chopped red bell pepper	30 mL
2 tbsp	chopped fresh parsley	30 mL

1. Heat 1 tbsp (15 mL) of oil with butter in a deep saucepan over medium heat, add ham and fry until ham begins to turn golden. Remove with a slotted spoon and set aside.

2. Add remaining oil to saucepan, stir in garlic, onion and mushrooms, and cook for 3 minutes. Add stock, crushed peppercorns and paprika. Mix well. Bring mixture to a boil, reduce heat and simmer for 10 minutes.

3. Stir in celery, lettuce, peas and pasta. Cook until vegetables are tender and pasta is *al dente*. Stir in ham, red pepper and parsley and serve.

Serves 4

Pork Ball and Broccoli Soup

8 cups	light chicken stock	2 L
2	leeks or 8 green onions, thinly sliced	2
1 tsp	finely chopped fresh ginger	5 mL
2 tbsp	rice wine or dry sherry	30 mL
1	head broccoli, stems thinly sliced, heads broken into florets	1
1	carrot, thinly sliced	1
	salt and freshly ground black pepper	

Meatballs

3/4 lb	lean ground pork	350 g
4	green onions, finely chopped	4
1 tsp	finely chopped fresh ginger	5 mL
1/2 tsp	salt	2 mL
1 tbsp	cornstarch	15 mL
1 tbsp	light soy sauce	15 mL
1	egg, beaten	1

♦ ♦ ♦

1. Place stock in a large saucepan and bring to a boil. Add leeks or green onions, ginger, wine or sherry, broccoli, carrot, and salt and black pepper to taste. Bring back to a boil. Lower heat and simmer for 5 minutes.

2. To make meatballs, place pork, green onions, ginger, salt, cornstarch, soy sauce and egg in a bowl and mix together until well combined.

3. Form into small, marble-sized balls and drop into simmering soup. Cook for 3-4 minutes longer or until meatballs are cooked through. Serve.

Serves 6

Chunky Meat and Chickpea Soup

2 tbsp	butter	30 mL
1 lb	beef or lamb fillet, cut into 3/4 inch (2 cm) cubes	450 g
1	large onion, chopped	1
1 tbsp	chopped fresh parsley	15 mL
2 tsp	paprika	10 mL
1 tsp	saffron powder	5 mL
1 tsp	coarsely ground black pepper	5 mL
6 cups	lamb or chicken stock	1.5 L
1/2 cup	dried chickpeas, soaked overnight in water	125 mL
1 lb	tomatoes, peeled, seeded and chopped	450 g
4 tbsp	lemon juice	60 mL
1/3 cup	long-grain rice	85 mL

♦ ♦ ♦

1. Melt butter in a large saucepan over medium heat. Add meat cubes, onion, parsley, paprika, saffron and pepper. Cook for 5 minutes, stirring frequently. Add stock.

2. Drain chickpeas and add them to pan with tomatoes and lemon juice. Bring to a boil, boil for 10 minutes, then cover pan and simmer for 1–1 1/4 hours.

3. Stir in rice. Cook for 15-20 minutes or until tender. Serve at once, in heated bowls.

Serves 6

TIP: If desired use butterbeans instead of chickpeas and substitute 2 sliced leeks for the onion. Or if you are in a hurry, use a can of drained canned chickpeas and canned tomatoes.

Curried Lamb Soup with Split Peas

2 tbsp	oil	30 mL
1 lb	meaty lamb bones, such as shanks or shoulder	450 g
3	garlic cloves, crushed	3
1	onion, finely chopped	1
2 tbsp	mild curry powder	30 mL
1 cup	yellow split peas, soaked overnight in water	250 mL
5 cups	boiling water	1.2 L
2 tbsp	chopped fresh mint	30 mL
2	carrots, finely diced	2
2	celery stalks, sliced	2
1/2 cup	coconut milk	125 mL
1 tbsp	lemon juice	15 mL
	salt	
	chopped chives for garnish	

1. Heat oil in a large saucepan over medium heat. Add lamb bones and brown on all sides. Add garlic, onion and curry powder and cook, stirring constantly, for 5 minutes. Drain peas and add them with boiling water. Bring to a boil, skim surface then lower heat. Simmer for 1 hour.

2. Remove lamb and slice meat on bones into small pieces. Set aside. Purée soup in a blender or food processor, return to clean pan and add mint, carrots and sliced lamb. Bring to a boil and cook until carrots are tender.

3. Stir in celery, coconut milk, lemon juice and salt to taste. Serve in heated bowls, garnished with chives.

Serves 4-6

TIP: Coconut milk adds rich flavor and a tropical aroma to soups and stews.

Spinach Soup with Sausage Meatballs

1 cup	dry white wine	250 mL
3 cups	chicken stock	750 mL
1 cup	drained canned tomatoes, chopped	250 mL
2	green onions, finely sliced	2
2 tbsp	tomato paste	30 mL
3/4 lb	pork sausage meat	350 g
2 tsp	dried mixed herbs (optional)	10 mL
1/4 lb	large mushrooms, sliced	110 g
2	drained canned pimientos, thinly sliced	2
1/4 lb	fresh leaf spinach, shredded	110 g

1. Boil wine in a saucepan until reduced by half. Lower heat and add stock, tomatoes, green onions and tomato paste. Bring to a boil, lower heat and simmer for 1 minute.

2. Roll sausage meat into small balls, adding herbs if desired. Add meatballs to soup and simmer for 7 minutes.

3. Stir in mushrooms, pimientos and spinach. Cook for 3 minutes or until vegetables are cooked to taste. Serve in heated bowls.

Serves 4

Hearty Beef and Brussels Sprout Soup

2 tbsp	oil	30 mL
1 lb	stewing beef, cut into 1 inch (2.5 cm) cubes	450 g
1	onion, chopped	1
3	garlic cloves, crushed	3
1/4 cup	dry sherry	60 mL
6 cups	chicken or beef stock	1.5 L
2/3 lb	new potatoes, sliced	300 g
1/4 lb	carrots, sliced	110 g
1 tsp	dried rosemary	5 mL
1/4 lb	Brussels sprouts, trimmed and halved	110 g
1/2 tsp	crushed black peppercorns	2 mL

♦ ♦ ♦

1. Heat oil in a large, deep saucepan over high heat. Add beef and stir until browned on all sides. Stir in onion and garlic and cook for 1 minute, then add sherry.

2. Pour stock into pan, bring to a boil, then simmer, partially covered, for 1 hour.

3. Add potatoes, carrots and rosemary and simmer for 10 minutes. Stir in Brussels sprouts and black pepper. Cook for 5 minutes or until sprouts are tender.

Serves 4

TIP: Try to use small, tender Brussels sprouts and avoid overcooking them or they will become strong-tasting as well as mushy. You could also substitute sliced green cabbage if you prefer.

Artichoke and Shrimp Bisque

4 tbsp	butter	60 mL
1	onion, chopped	1
2	potatoes, cut into 1/2 inch (1 cm) cubes	2
14 oz	can artichoke hearts, drained	398 mL
3 cups	milk	750 mL
1/2 tsp	paprika	2 mL
1/4 tsp	freshly ground black pepper	1 mL
1/2 lb	peeled cooked shrimp	225 g
	chopped chives for garnish	

♦ ♦ ♦

1 Melt butter in a large saucepan. Add onion and potato and cook gently for 5 minutes.

2 Stir in artichoke hearts, milk, paprika and pepper. Bring soup to a boil, lower heat and simmer for 20 minutes.

3 Purée soup in a blender or food processor, return to a clean pan and heat gently.

4 When ready to serve, bring soup to a boil. Set aside a few shrimp for garnish and add remainder to soup. As soon as they have heated through, ladle soup into heated bowls. Garnish with chives and reserved shrimp.

Serves 4

Easy French Onion Soup

4 tbsp	butter	60 mL
5	onions, finely chopped	5
2	beef stock cubes, crumbled	2
4 cups	water	1 L
1	loaf French bread, cut into 12 slices	1
2-3 tsp	Dijon mustard	10-15 mL
1/2 cup	old Cheddar cheese, grated	125 mL
3 tbsp	brandy	45 mL
	salt and freshly ground black pepper	

♦ ♦ ♦

1 Melt butter in a large saucepan. Add onions and cook over low heat, stirring occasionally, until golden brown.

2 Add stock cubes and cook, stirring frequently, for 3 minutes. Stir in water, bring to a boil, then simmer for about 30 minutes.

3 Toast French bread on both sides. Spread mustard on one side of each slice and top with grated cheese. Broil until melted.

4 Taste soup and season with salt and pepper. Stir in brandy. Serve in heated bowls, placing two or three slices of cheese toast on each portion.

Serves 4

TIP: Do not hurry the process of frying the onions. Long, slow cooking ensures maximum flavor. For a richer flavor, use homemade beef stock or canned beef broth instead of the water and stock cubes.

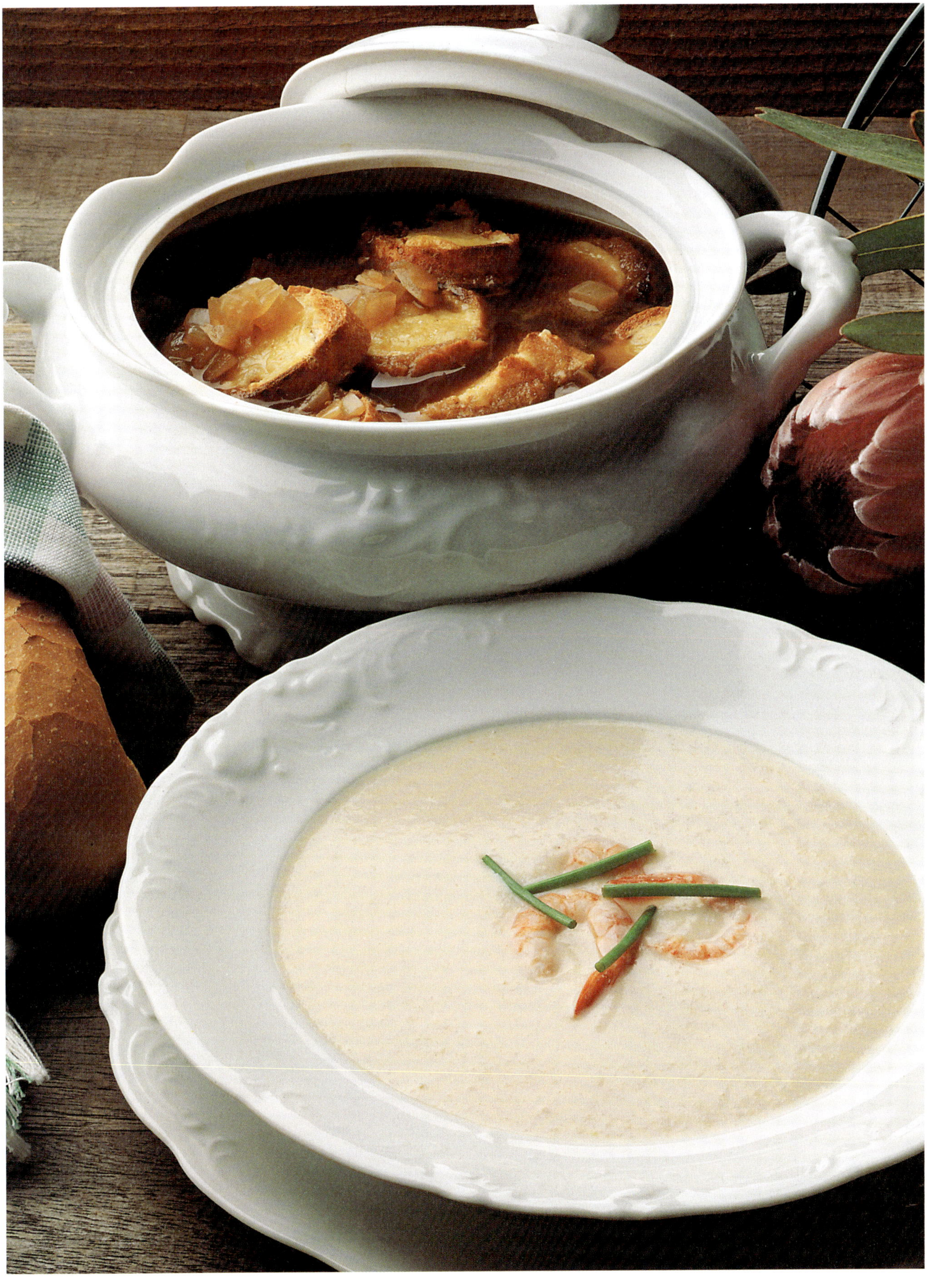

Smoked Salmon Soup

3 cups	fish stock, see Tip	750 mL
1/2 cup	light cream	125 mL
1 cup	milk	250 mL
1/2 tsp	grated nutmeg	2 mL
1/4 lb	smoked salmon, cut into thin strips	110 g
	chopped chives for garnish	
	salt and freshly ground black pepper	

◆ ◆ ◆

1 Bring stock to a boil. Lower heat and stir in cream, milk and nutmeg. Season to taste. Set aside a little salmon for garnish, and add the rest to the soup. Heat through gently without boiling. Serve in heated bowls, garnished with reserved salmon and chives.

Serves 4

TIP: To make fish stock, put fish trimmings (including head and bones, but not the gills, which will make the stock bitter) in a saucepan. Add 1/2 onion, 1 sliced celery stalk, 4 white peppercorns, 1/2 tsp (2 mL) salt and a bouquet garni. Add 2 1/2 cups (625 mL) water. Bring to a boil, simmer for 30 minutes, strain and use.

Tomato and Shellfish Soup

2 tbsp	olive oil	30 mL
2	onions, cut into rings	2
8	large tomatoes, chopped	8
2	garlic cloves, crushed	2
1 tsp	crushed black peppercorns	5 mL
1 tbsp	chopped fresh oregano	15 mL
1 tbsp	chopped fresh parsley	15 mL
1 tbsp	chopped fresh basil	15 mL
3 cups	chicken stock	750 mL
1/2 cup	tomato paste	125 mL
5 oz	vermicelli noodles	150 g
1/2 lb	assorted shellfish, cooked	225 g

◆ ◆ ◆

1. Heat oil in a large deep skillet, add onions and cook for 3 minutes. Add tomatoes, garlic, crushed peppercorns, oregano, parsley and basil and simmer until tomatoes are soft.

2. Add 2 cups (500 mL) of chicken stock to tomato mixture and bring to a boil. Reduce heat and simmer for 30 minutes. Push mixture through a sieve into a large saucepan.

3. Stir in remaining stock and tomato paste to mixture, bring to a boil, add vermicelli and cook until pasta is *al dente*. Stir in shellfish just before serving.

Serves 4-6

TIP: *Clams, mussels, shrimp, crayfish or whatever else strikes your fancy are all good in this soup, but each type should be cooked separately so that nothing is overcooked.*

Tuscan Bean Soup

3/4 cup	dried red kidney beans, soaked overnight in water	185 mL
4 cups	unsalted vegetable stock or water	1 L
1/2 cup	olive oil	125 mL
2	carrots, chopped	2
2	celery stalks, sliced	2
4	zucchini, chopped	4
2 cups	chopped canned tomatoes	500 mL
2 tsp	dried basil	10 mL
3	garlic cloves, crushed	3
5 cups	chicken stock	1.2 L
4 cups	chopped cabbage	1 L
	salt and pepper to taste	

1. Drain beans, put in a saucepan and add vegetable stock or water. Bring to a boil and boil vigorously for 10 minutes. Lower heat and simmer for 1 hour; drain.

2. Heat oil in a saucepan, add carrots, celery and zucchini and fry for 4 minutes over medium-high heat. Stir in tomatoes, basil and garlic and cook for 10 minutes, stirring constantly.

3. Add chicken stock and beans. Bring to a boil, then simmer for 30 minutes. Add cabbage and cook for 2 minutes more. Season to taste before serving.

Serves 6-8

♦ ♦ ♦

Mushroom Vegetable Soup

1/2 cup	olive oil	125 mL
6	slices bacon, finely chopped	6
1/4 lb	mushrooms, sliced	110 g
1	onion, finely chopped	1
5 cups	chicken stock	1.2 L
2	potatoes, cut into tiny cubes	2
2	carrots, cut into tiny cubes	2
2 tbsp	chopped fresh parsley	30 mL
1/2 tsp	coarsely ground black pepper	2 mL

1. Heat oil in a skillet over medium-high heat. Add bacon, mushrooms and onion. Cook for 5 minutes, stirring occasionally.

2. Bring stock to a boil in a large saucepan. Add potatoes, carrots and bacon mixture. Simmer for 10 minutes or until vegetables are tender. Serve sprinkled with parsley and black pepper.

Serves 6

♦ ♦ ♦

27

Carrot Soup with Coriander

4 tbsp	butter	60 mL
4	green onions, finely chopped	4
4 tbsp	chopped fresh coriander	60 mL
4 cups	chicken stock	1 L
1 tsp	coarsely ground black pepper	5 mL
1 lb	carrots, chopped	450 g
1	large potato, chopped	1
¼ cup	whipping cream	60 mL
3 tbsp	chopped fresh parsley	45 mL

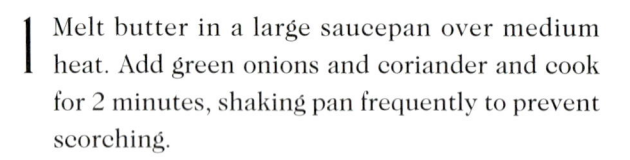

1. Melt butter in a large saucepan over medium heat. Add green onions and coriander and cook for 2 minutes, shaking pan frequently to prevent scorching.

2. Add stock, pepper, carrots and potato. Bring to a boil, then lower heat and simmer soup for 20 minutes or until vegetables are tender.

3. Purée vegetables and stock in a blender or food processor until smooth. Return soup to a clean saucepan and heat through.

4. Ladle into heated soup bowls. Drizzle 1 tbsp (15 mL) of cream into each portion, sprinkle with chopped parsley and serve at once, with crusty bread or one of the sandwiches on page 70.

Serves 4

TIP: When time is short, grate the carrots and potatoes for speedy cooking. The fresh coriander gives a distinctive flavor which may not be to everyone's taste. If you're not a coriander fan, try flavoring carrot soup with a little grated fresh ginger instead.

Mixed Vegetable Soup

2 tbsp	butter	30 mL
1	onion, sliced	1
6	new potatoes, sliced	6
6 cups	chicken stock	1.5 L
2	carrots, cut into matchsticks	2
2	zucchini, sliced	2
1 1/2	small eggplants, diced	1 1/2
1 1/2 cups	frozen peas, thawed	375 mL
1/2	red bell pepper, cut into strips	1/2
1/2	green bell pepper, cut into strips	1/2
3 tbsp	chopped fresh parsley	45 mL
1/2 tsp	coarsely ground black pepper	2 mL

♦ ♦ ♦

1. Melt butter in a large saucepan over medium heat. Add onion and potatoes and cook, stirring frequently, for 5 minutes.

2. Add stock. Bring to a boil, then lower heat and simmer for 5 minutes.

3. Add carrots, zucchini, eggplant, peas, red and green pepper strips, parsley and pepper. Cook for 10-12 minutes, or until vegetables are tender. Serve in heated bowls.

Serves 4

TIP: *Use good quality homemade chicken stock for this soup if possible. Vegetable stock may be used instead, with a 1/2 tsp (2 mL) of yeast extract or marmite stirred in for extra flavor.*

BASIL AND ALMOND SOUP

Basil and Almond Soup

4 tbsp	vegetable oil	60 mL
1	onion, chopped	1
2	garlic cloves, crushed	2
1/4 cup	slivered almonds	60 mL
4 cups	chicken stock	1 L
1/4 tsp	crushed black peppercorns	1 mL
4 tbsp	chopped fresh basil	60 mL
1/3 lb	spaghetti, broken into pieces	150 g

1. Heat oil in a large saucepan over low heat. Add onion, garlic and almonds, and cook until onions are transparent.

2. Stir in stock, crushed peppercorns and basil, cover saucepan and simmer for 10 minutes.

3. Bring a large saucepan of water to a boil, add spaghetti and cook until *al dente*. Drain pasta and add to soup.

4. Serve immediately, topped with grated cheese, if desired.

Serves 4

Classic Leek and Potato Soup

3 tbsp	butter	45 mL
3	large potatoes, chopped	3
6	leeks, thinly sliced	6
2	onions, thinly sliced	2
6 cups	chicken stock	1.5 L
2 cups	light cream	500 mL
1	bunch chives, finely chopped	1
2 tbsp	chopped fresh parsley	30 mL
	salt and freshly ground black pepper	
	croûtons (optional)	

1. Melt butter in a heavy-based saucepan, add potatoes, leeks and onions and cook over low heat for 5 minutes.

2. Add chicken stock. Bring to a boil, then lower heat and simmer, covered, until all vegetables are tender. Cool.

3. Purée soup in a blender or food processor. Return to a clean pan, stir in cream and heat through gently. Do not allow soup to boil.

4. Add chives and parsley and stir in salt and pepper to taste. Serve in heated bowls, garnishing each portion with croûtons.

Serves 6

Minestrone with Pesto

1 tbsp	butter	15 mL
1/2	onion, chopped	1/2
1	leek, sliced	1
1	carrot, sliced	1
1	celery stalk, sliced	1
1	garlic clove, crushed	1
2	tomatoes, chopped	2
4	cabbage leaves, chopped	4
1 cup	sliced green beans	250 mL
6 cups	chicken stock	1.5 L
1/3 cup	grated Pecorino or Parmesan cheese	85 mL
	salt and pepper to taste	

PESTO

1 cup	packed fresh basil leaves	250 mL
6	large garlic cloves, crushed	6
1 tbsp	olive oil	15 mL

1. To make pesto, place basil leaves, garlic cloves and oil in a blender and process until mixture is very finely chopped. Pour mixture into an ice cube tray and freeze until ready to use.

2. To make minestrone, melt butter in a very large saucepan over medium heat. Add onion, leek, carrot, celery, garlic, tomatoes, cabbage and beans, and cook for 2 minutes, stirring constantly. Add stock and bring to a boil. Lower heat and simmer, uncovered, for 20 minutes.

3. Serve soup in large heated bowls. Place a pesto cube in each bowl and sprinkle with cheese.

Serves 6

TIP: For a richer pesto, add 1/2 cup (125 mL) of pine nuts or walnuts to the mixture before processing.

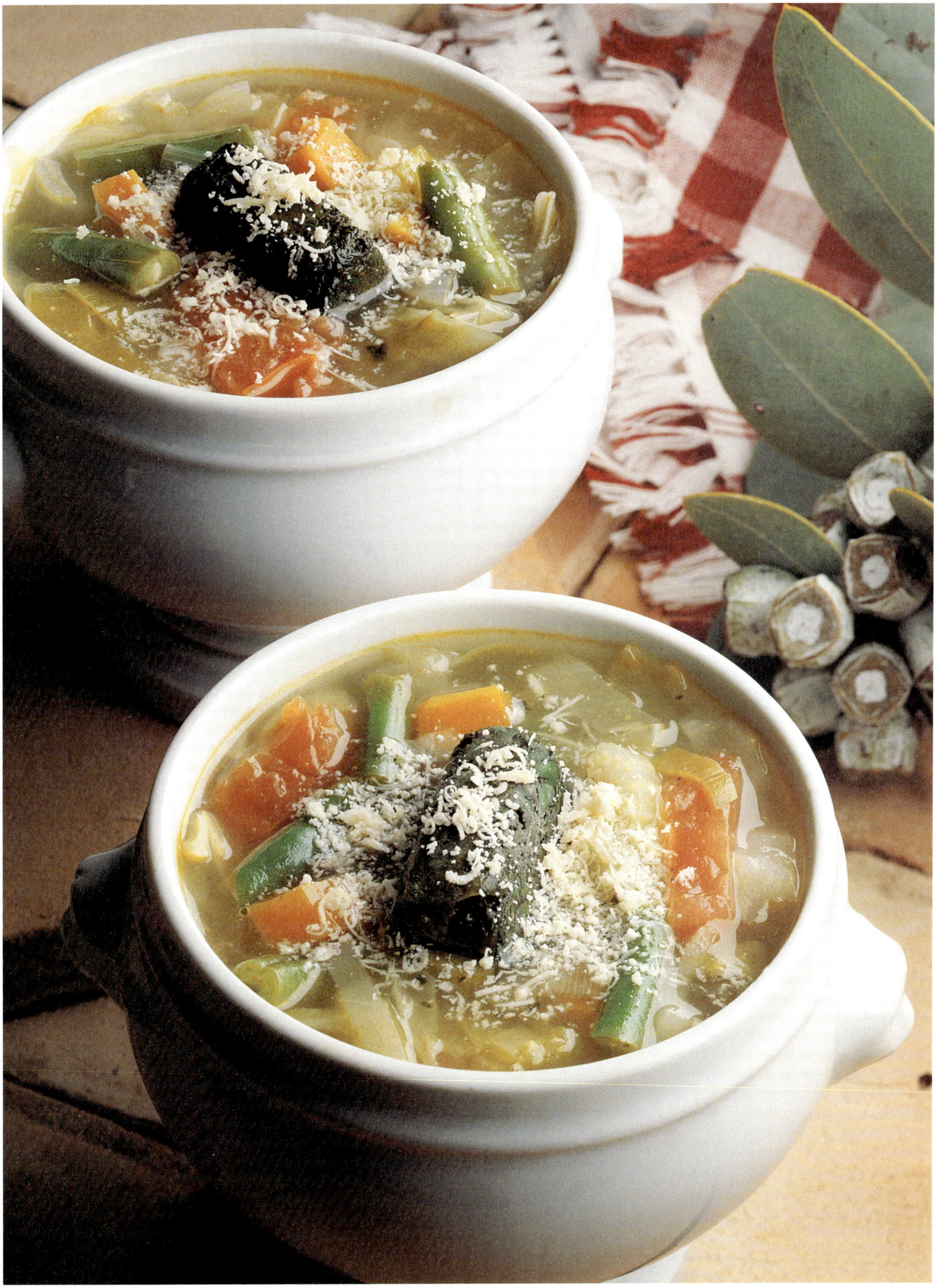

Chilled Roasted Red Pepper Soup

6	medium red bell peppers	6
4 tbsp	butter	60 mL
2	leeks, white part only, sliced	2
2	garlic cloves, crushed	2
2 tbsp	tomato paste	30 mL
2 cups	chicken stock	500 mL
1 cup	plain low-fat yogurt	250 mL
½ cup	whipping cream	125 mL

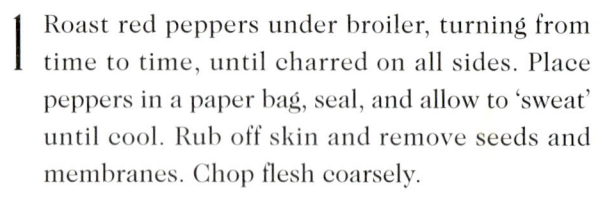

◆ ◆ ◆

1. Roast red peppers under broiler, turning from time to time, until charred on all sides. Place peppers in a paper bag, seal, and allow to 'sweat' until cool. Rub off skin and remove seeds and membranes. Chop flesh coarsely.

2. Melt butter in a large saucepan over medium heat. Add leeks and garlic and sauté for 3-5 minutes until softened but not browned.

3. Stir in red peppers, tomato paste and chicken stock. Bring to a boil, lower heat and simmer soup for 20 minutes. Set aside to cool to room temperature.

4. Purée soup in a blender or food processor until smooth. Transfer to a bowl, stir in yogurt and cream, cover and chill for 3 hours before serving.

Serves 4

TIP: This unusual soup can also be served hot. Reheat the puréed red pepper mixture gently with yogurt. Swirl the cream on top to serve.

Mulligatawny Soup

2 tbsp	olive oil	30 mL
3	celery stalks, chopped	3
2	small zucchini, unpeeled, chopped	2
1/2	onion, chopped	1/2
1 tbsp	all-purpose flour	15 mL
1 1/2 tsp	curry powder	7 mL
3 cups	chicken stock	750 mL
1/4 lb	boneless chicken breast meat, diced	110 g
1 cup	cooked white rice	250 mL
1	apple, unpeeled, diced	1
2 tsp	finely chopped fresh coriander (optional)	10 mL
	salt and freshly ground pepper	

1. Heat oil in a saucepan, add celery, zucchini and onion, and cook over medium heat until tender, stirring occasionally. Add flour and curry powder, stir well to combine, and cook 1 minute.

2. Add stock and chicken and bring to a boil. Lower heat and let simmer 15 minutes.

3. Add rice and apple. Simmer another 15 minutes to blend flavors. Season to taste. Sprinkle with fresh coriander if desired and serve.

Serves 4

TIP: This is a handy recipe for using leftover cooked chicken, in which case add the diced chicken with the rice. Vary the vegetables to use what you have on hand. Even carrots and potatoes get a boost from the curry treatment!

Potato Soup with Croûtons

3 tbsp	butter	45 mL
1	onion, chopped	1
2	garlic cloves, crushed	2
4	large potatoes, chopped	4
1	leek, sliced	1
3 cups	chicken stock	750 mL
1/2 tsp	grated nutmeg	2 mL
1 cup	light cream	250 mL
4	slices thick white bread, crusts removed, cut into small strips	4
	salt and pepper to taste	
	oil for shallow frying	
	chopped chives for garnish	

1. Melt butter in a large saucepan over medium heat. Add onion and garlic and cook for 3-5 minutes until softened. Add potatoes, leek, chicken stock and nutmeg. Simmer for 20 minutes, or until vegetables are tender. Season to taste.

2. Purée soup, in batches, in a blender or food processor. Return soup to a clean saucepan. Stir in cream and mix well. Heat through without boiling.

3. Meanwhile, heat oil in a large skillet over medium heat. Add bread strips and cook for 2 minutes, turning frequently. Drain on paper towels. Serve soup in heated bowls, garnished with croûtons and chives.

Serves 4

Vegetarian Soups

Vegetarians have the pick of the crop when it comes to soups. Take fresh country vegetables, a few carefully chosen herbs and spices, and what have you got? Quite simply — pots of flavor.

One of the advantages of selecting a vegetarian soup is that it eliminates the need to make a homemade meat stock or purchase a canned version. But when you taste a hearty mushroom and barley soup or savoury green minestrone, you won't think anything's missing!

FENNEL SOUP (PAGE 38)

Fennel Soup

2 tbsp	olive oil	30 mL
1	onion, sliced	1
1	garlic clove, crushed	1
4	fennel bulbs	4
2 cups	chopped canned tomatoes	500 mL
2 tbsp	tomato paste	30 mL
4 cups	vegetable stock	1 L
	salt and freshly ground black pepper	

1. Heat oil in a large saucepan. Add onion and garlic and cook over low heat for 5 minutes, stirring occasionally.

2. Halve fennel bulbs. Set aside feathery tops for garnish; slice fennel thinly. Add to pan with tomatoes. Stir in tomato paste and cook for 5 minutes over medium heat.

3. Add stock. Bring to a boil, lower heat and simmer, covered, for 30 minutes. Add salt and pepper to taste.

4. Ladle soup into heated bowls, garnish with fennel tops and serve with toasted Italian bread.

Serves 4

Chestnut Soup

1/4 lb	butter	110 g
1	onion, coarsely chopped	1
2	carrots, coarsely chopped	2
4 tbsp	all-purpose flour	60 mL
8 cups	vegetable stock	2 L
16 oz	canned chestnuts, drained	450 g
1 cup	light cream (optional)	250 mL
	salt and freshly ground black pepper	

1. Melt butter in a saucepan. Add onion and carrots and cook over low heat for 5 minutes.

2. Stir in flour and cook for 1 minute. Raise heat and gradually add stock, stirring until mixture thickens slightly. Add chestnuts. Season with salt and pepper to taste. Simmer, uncovered, for 30 minutes.

3. Purée soup. Return to a clean pan, add cream if desired, and reheat gently. Serve in heated bowls.

Serves 8

Mushroom and Barley Soup

1 lb	fresh mushrooms, sliced	450 g
1	small tomato, quartered	1
2	carrots, chopped	2
1	onion, chopped	1
2	celery stalks, chopped	2
1/2 tsp	salt	2 mL
4	parsley sprigs, chopped	4
1/2 cup	pearl barley	125 mL
6 cups	water	1.5 L
	chopped fresh parsley for garnish	

1. In a large saucepan combine mushrooms, tomato, carrots, onion, celery, salt, parsley sprigs, barley and water.

2. Bring to a boil, reduce heat and simmer covered for 1 hour, or until barley is tender. Serve hot, garnished with fresh parsley.

Serves 4

Leek Soup with Thyme

2 tbsp	butter	30 mL
¾ lb	leeks, white part only, chopped	350 g
2	potatoes, chopped	2
2 tsp	chopped fresh thyme	10 mL
4 cups	vegetable stock	1 L
4 tbsp	light cream	60 mL
	fresh thyme for garnish	

♦ ♦ ♦

1. Melt butter in a large saucepan over medium heat. Add leeks and cook for 2 minutes. Add potatoes and thyme; toss to coat in butter.

2. Add stock. Bring to a boil, then simmer until potatoes are tender. Purée mixture, return to clean pan and heat through.

3. Serve soup in heated bowls. Spoon 1 tbsp (15 mL) of cream onto center of each portion, then swirl cream with a skewer. Garnish with fresh thyme.

Serves 4

TIP: Food processors and blenders make cream soups a snap to make. Remember than you can also shorten cooking time for the vegetables by using your food processor to coarsely chop your ingredients.

Green Minestrone

4 tbsp	butter	60 mL
1/2 lb	fresh asparagus	225 g
1 lb	broccoli	450 g
4	green onions, chopped	4
1 cup	broad beans, fresh or frozen	250 mL
1 1/2 cups	peas, fresh or frozen	375 mL
2	vegetable stock cubes	2
1 cup	green beans	250 mL

♦ ♦ ♦

1 Melt butter in a large saucepan over medium heat. Set aside asparagus tips; chop stalks and add them to pan.

2 Set aside broccoli florets for use in another recipe; chop stems and add them to pan with green onions, broad beans and most of the peas. Toss lightly to mix; cook until just softened.

3 Crumble in stock cubes. Add enough water to cover vegetables by 1 inch (2.5 cm). Bring to a boil, lower heat and simmer until all vegetables are tender.

4 Purée soup in several batches in a blender or food processor. Return purée to clean pan, add reserved asparagus tips, remaining peas and green beans and cook for 5 minutes. Ladle soup into heated bowls, sprinkle with grated cheese, if desired, and serve with fresh bread rolls.

Serves 4

Old-Fashioned Pumpkin Soup

Old-Fashioned Pumpkin Soup

2 tbsp	butter	30 mL
1	large onion, chopped	1
2 lbs	pumpkin, cubed	1 kg
3 1/2 cups	vegetable stock	900 mL
1/2 tsp	grated nutmeg	2 mL
1/2 cup	evaporated milk	125 mL
	salt and freshly ground black pepper	

♦ ♦ ♦

1. Melt butter in a large saucepan. Add onion and cook for 3-4 minutes, until golden. Add pumpkin cubes and cook for 2 minutes more, stirring constantly.

2. Add stock and nutmeg. Bring to a boil, then simmer until pumpkin is tender.

3. Purée soup in batches. Return to a clean pan and stir in evaporated milk. Season with salt and pepper and more nutmeg, if desired. Reheat without boiling.

Serves 4-6

TIP: Substitute any variety of winter squash for the pumpkin in this recipe.

Garlic Soup

3 tbsp	olive oil	45 mL
2-3	garlic cloves, crushed	2-3
4	slices bread, crusts removed, crumbled	4
1/2 tsp	cayenne pepper	2 mL
6 cups	vegetable stock	1.5 L
2	celery stalks, cut into matchsticks	2
1	parsnip, cut into matchsticks	1
2	eggs, beaten	2
3 tbsp	chopped fresh parsley	45 mL
	salt and freshly ground black pepper	

♦ ♦ ♦

1. Heat oil in a saucepan over medium heat. Add garlic, lower heat and cook for 2 minutes. Do not let garlic burn. Add bread and fry until golden. Stir in cayenne.

2. Add stock and bring to a boil. Lower heat and simmer for 20 minutes. Add vegetable matchsticks. Cook for 2 minutes.

3. Add eggs and parsley to simmering soup. Stir over medium heat until eggs form threads. Season to taste and serve at once.

Serves 4

Creamy Mushroom Soup

4 tbsp	butter	60 mL
1	large onion, sliced	1
4 cups	sliced mushrooms	1 L
1 tbsp	chopped fresh chervil	15 mL
2 cups	vegetable stock	500 mL
2 tbsp	cornstarch	30 mL
1 cup	milk	250 mL
½ cup	whipping cream	125 mL

1. Melt butter in a large saucepan. Add onion and mushrooms; sauté for 5 minutes.

2. Add chervil and stock. Simmer for 20 minutes. Purée in a blender or food processor. Return mixture to a clean pan.

3. In a cup, mix cornstarch with a little milk into a paste. Add to mushroom purée with remaining milk. Stir over medium heat until soup boils and thickens. Remove pan from heat, and stir in cream. Serve at once, garnished as desired.

Serves 4

Dilled Carrot and Sweet Potato Soup

2 tbsp	butter	30 mL
1	large onion, chopped	1
1	large sweet potato, chopped	1
3	large carrots, sliced	3
4 cups	vegetable stock	1 L
¾ cup	sour cream	185 mL
2 tbsp	chopped fresh dill	30 mL

♦ ♦ ♦

1. Melt butter in a saucepan. Add onion, sweet potato and carrots; sauté for 5 minutes.

2. Stir in vegetable stock. Bring to a boil, lower heat and simmer for 30 minutes or until vegetables are tender.

3. Purée mixture with sour cream. Return to a clean pan and reheat gently without boiling. Stir in dill and serve at once in heated bowls.

Serves 4

Hearty Bean and Vegetable Soup

1 cup	dried small white beans, soaked overnight in water	250 mL
1 tbsp	oil	15 mL
2	onions, chopped	2
2	garlic cloves, crushed	2
2	carrots, sliced	2
2	celery stalks, sliced	2
2	potatoes, chopped	2
2 cups	chopped canned tomatoes	500 mL
6 cups	water	1.5 L
2 tbsp	chopped parsley for garnish	30 mL
	salt and pepper to taste	

1. Drain beans. Bring a large saucepan of water to a boil, add beans and boil vigorously for 10 minutes, then simmer for 30-40 minutes more or until tender. Drain, reserving 2 cups (500 mL) of cooking liquid. Purée half of the beans with reserved cooking liquid. Set aside with remaining beans.

2. Heat oil in a saucepan, add onions and garlic and fry until tender. Add carrots, celery, potatoes, tomatoes with can juices, 6 cups (1.5 L) water, beans and bean purée. Bring to a boil, then simmer, covered, for 20 minutes or until vegetables are tender. Season to taste, stir in parsley and serve.

Serves 4

Miso Soup

2 tbsp	olive oil	30 mL
1	onion, chopped	1
1	garlic clove, crushed	1
1	celery stalk	1
1	carrot, chopped	1
1	parsnip, chopped	1
1	sweet potato, diced	1
1 cup	winter squash	250 mL
1 cup	corn, frozen or canned and drained	250 mL
2 cups	vegetable stock	500 mL
8 tsp	miso	40 mL

1. Heat oil in a large saucepan. Add onion and garlic and cook over low heat for 5 minutes, stirring occasionally.

2. Add celery, carrot, parsnip, sweet potato, squash and corn. Cook for 5 minutes, stirring occasionally.

3. Add stock. Bring to a boil, lower heat and simmer, covered, for 30 minutes, or until vegetables are tender.

4. Place 2 tsp (10 mL) miso in each of four heated soup bowls. Ladle in hot soup and serve.

Serves 4

TIP: *Miso is a richly flavored Japanese paste made from fermented soy beans. Add at the last minute, as cooking reduces its nutritional value.*

Hearty Bean and Vegetable Soup

Fruity Spinach Soup

2 tbsp	butter	30 mL
1	onion, chopped	1
1	garlic clove, crushed	1
2 lbs	spinach, washed, trimmed and coarsely chopped	1 kg
½ cup	unsweetened apple juice	125 mL
½ cup	freshly squeezed orange juice	125 mL
1 cup	vegetable stock	250 mL
1 tsp	grated fresh ginger	5 mL
1 tsp	cornstarch	5 mL
½ cup	plain low-fat yogurt	125 mL

♦ ♦ ♦

1. Melt butter in a large saucepan, add onion and garlic and cook over low heat for 5 minutes.

2. Add spinach, apple juice, orange juice, stock and ginger to pan. Bring to a boil, lower heat and simmer, covered, for 20 minutes.

3. Purée soup in several batches in a blender or food processor. Return it to a clean saucepan. In a cup, mix cornstarch and yogurt to a thin cream consistency; pour mixture into pan and mix well.

4. Just before serving, reheat soup gently, stirring constantly. Do not allow it to boil. Serve in heated bowls, garnished with a drizzle of cream and a sprinkle of chopped parsley if desired.

Serves 4

Mediterranean Vegetable and Pasta Soup

1 cup	dried white beans	250 mL
6 cups	vegetable stock	1.5 L
1 ½ cups	sliced mushrooms	375 mL
1 cup	chopped green beans	250 mL
2	carrots, chopped	2
2	small yellow summer squash or zucchini, sliced	2
1	leek, sliced	1
5 oz	small shell pasta	150 g
1 tsp	crushed black peppercorns	5 mL
1 cup	chopped canned tomatoes	250 mL

♦ ♦ ♦

1. Soak beans for 8 hours in 4 cups (1 L) water.

2. Rinse and drain beans, then combine them with stock in a large saucepan. Bring to a boil, boil for 5 minutes, then simmer, covered, for 1 hour or until tender.

3. Add mushrooms to cooked beans, then add green beans, carrots, squash or zucchini and leek.

4. Add 2 cups (500 mL) water, bring to a boil and simmer covered for 30 minutes. Add pasta, crushed peppercorns and tomatoes, and cook until vegetables are tender and pasta is *al dente*.

Serves 6-8

TIP: *You can vary the vegetables according to what you have on hand. A little pesto may be stirred into the soup at the end.*

Cool Summer Soups

When summer sizzles, what better way to start a meal than with a bowl of chilled soup? Whether your choice is cool green avocado, rich red gazpacho or smooth chilled butternut, simple summer soups are sure to be popular.

Because most cold soups are puréed, they benefit especially from the use of garnishes to provide texture or color contrast. Take a look at the garnish ideas on page 61. Time spent on preparing a garnish will be amply repaid when family or friends survey — and sample — the results.

CHILLED TOMATO AND AVOCADO SOUP (PAGE 52)

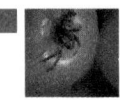

Chilled Tomato and Avocado Soup

2 tbsp	butter	30 mL
2	green onions, chopped	2
1	garlic clove, crushed	1
2 cups	chopped canned tomatoes	500 mL
2	medium avocados, halved, pitted, peeled and chopped	2
1 1/2 cups	chicken stock	375 mL
1/2 cup	plain low-fat yogurt	125 mL
1 tbsp	lemon juice	15 mL
1/4 tsp	freshly ground black pepper	1 mL

◆ ◆ ◆

1. Melt butter in a saucepan over medium heat. Add green onions and garlic and cook, stirring, for 1 minute.

2. Stir in tomatoes and avocados. Cook, stirring constantly, for 5 minutes. Stir in stock and simmer for 5 minutes.

3. Purée mixture in a blender or food processor, transfer to a bowl and allow to cool. Stir in yogurt, lemon juice and pepper. Mix thoroughly. Chill. Garnish with fresh herbs to serve.

Serves 4

TIP: *Taste the soup just before serving. Add a little more lemon juice, or salt and pepper to sharpen the flavor if desired.*

Borscht

1 lb	raw beets, peeled and roughly grated	450 g
1	onion, finely chopped	1
5 cups	beef stock	1.2 L
1	bay leaf	1
2 tbsp	tomato paste	30 mL
1 tbsp	lemon juice	15 mL
	salt and freshly ground black pepper	
	pinch of sugar	
	sour cream or plain yogurt to garnish	

◆ ◆ ◆

1. Combine beets, onion and stock in a saucepan. Add bay leaf. Bring to a boil, lower heat and simmer for 45 minutes.

2. Stir in tomato paste and lemon juice, with salt, pepper and sugar to taste. Cook for 15 minutes more.

3. Strain soup, pressing vegetables with a wooden spoon to extract as much flavor as possible. Let cool then refrigerate soup until required. Serve chilled, garnished with sour cream or yogurt.

Serves 4-6

TIP: *This light, clear version of the classic Russian soup is served chilled, with sour cream. For a hot soup, add 1/2 lb (225 g) diced steak with the beets, and about 1/4 lb (110 g) shredded cabbage with the tomato paste. Do not strain the soup, but remember to remove the bay leaf.*

Chilled Butternut Soup

1	onion, sliced	1
4 tbsp	butter	60 mL
1 ½ lbs	butternut squash, chopped	675 g
4	thin slices lemon, seeds removed	4
4 tbsp	all-purpose flour	60 mL
6 cups	warm chicken stock	1.5 L
1 cup	whipping cream, chilled	250 mL
	salt and freshly ground white pepper	
	lemon juice to taste	
	chopped fresh chives for garnish	

♦ ♦ ♦

1. Cook onion gently in butter in a large saucepan until soft. Stir in squash and lemon slices, sprinkle with flour and stir over low heat for 3 minutes. Remove from heat and cool a little, then add chicken stock, stirring until blended.

2. Return to heat and bring to a boil, stirring constantly. Season lightly with salt and white pepper and simmer, partially covered, for 30 minutes. Discard lemon slices. Purée mixture in a blender or food processor and pour into a bowl. Allow to cool, then refrigerate, covered, for at least 4 hours.

3. Stir in chilled cream and lemon juice. Adjust seasonings and serve in chilled bowls sprinkled with chives.

Serves 6-8

Chilled Apple and Fennel Soup

3 tbsp	butter	45 mL
2	onions, sliced	2
1	large fennel bulb, trimmed and sliced, feathery leaves reserved	1
3	Granny Smith apples, chopped	3
1 1/2 cups	chicken stock	375 mL
1 tbsp	chopped chives	15 mL
2/3 cup	plain low-fat yogurt	165 mL
	salt and pepper to taste	

♦ ♦ ♦

1 Melt butter in a large saucepan over medium heat. Add onions, fennel and apples. Cook, stirring constantly, for 3 minutes.

2 Pour in stock and add chives. Simmer for about 30 minutes, or until vegetables are very soft.

3 Blend or process mixture until smooth. Let cool, then stir in yogurt. Chill. Season to taste and serve garnished with fennel leaves.

Serves 4

Tomato Dill Soup

2-3 tbsp	light olive oil	30-45 mL
2	large onions, peeled and sliced	2
2	garlic cloves, crushed	2
1	handful fresh dill, finely chopped	1
6 cups	chicken stock	1.5 L
3 lbs	tomatoes, coarsely chopped	1.5 kg
2 tsp	finely grated orange rind	10 mL
	salt and freshly ground black pepper	
	pinch of sugar	
	dill sprigs, diced cucumber and diced bell peppers for garnish	

1 Heat oil in a large saucepan, add onions and cook gently for 20 minutes or until tender. Add garlic and cook 3-5 minutes. Add dill and season with salt and black pepper; cook for 15 minutes. Add chicken stock, tomatoes and sugar. Bring to a boil, reduce heat, cover and simmer for 30 minutes.

2 Push soup through a sieve. Add orange rind and set aside to cool. Chill for several hours or overnight before serving.

3 Taste and check for seasoning — it may need more after chilling. Ladle soup into bowls and garnish with dill, cucumber and peppers.

Serves 4

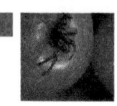

Gazpacho

2 tbsp	day-old white breadcrumbs	30 mL
2	garlic cloves, crushed	2
1 tbsp	red wine vinegar	15 mL
1 tbsp	olive oil	15 mL
1	green bell pepper, seeded and chopped	1
1	onion, coarsely chopped	1
5	ripe tomatoes, peeled, seeded and coarsely chopped	5
1	cucumber, peeled and coarsely chopped	1
2 tbsp	ground almonds	30 mL
4 tbsp	tomato paste	60 mL
1 tbsp	chopped fresh parsley	15 mL
	salt and pepper to to taste	

1. Put breadcrumbs and garlic in a small bowl. Add vinegar and olive oil. Mix well, cover bowl and set aside for 2 hours.

2. Combine green pepper, onion, tomatoes, cucumber, almonds, tomato paste and breadcrumb mixture in a blender or food processor. Process briefly, until vegetables are just chopped.

3. Transfer mixture to a large chilled bowl and stir in enough ice water to give soup consistency of light cream. Cover bowl; chill. Season to taste, and serve topped with chopped parsley.

Serves 4

TIP: *In Spain it is customary to offer bowls of croûtons, chopped olives, diced onion, diced cucumber, diced bell pepper, and finely chopped hard-boiled egg to accompany gazpacho. It is sometimes served with ice cubes floating on top of soup.*

Chilled Indian Cucumber Soup

1	bunch fresh coriander	1
2	onions, roughly chopped	2
4	cucumbers, peeled, seeded and sliced	4
2 ½ cups	plain low-fat yogurt	625 mL
1 tsp	curry powder	5 mL
4	drops Tabasco sauce	4
2 cups	skimmed chicken stock	500 mL
5 tbsp	plain low-fat yogurt	75 mL
	salt and freshly ground black pepper	
	coriander leaves for garnish	

1. Wash coriander thoroughly. Chop leaves and stalks in a food processor. Add onions and cucumbers and process until finely chopped.

2. In a large bowl combine yogurt with curry powder and Tabasco. Season to taste with salt and freshly ground pepper.

3. Whisk chicken stock and cucumber mixture into yogurt. Cover and refrigerate for at least 2 hours.

4. Serve in chilled bowls and garnish with a dollop of yogurt and fresh coriander leaves.

Serves 8

GAZPACHO

Chilled Watercress and Lemon Soup

2	bunches watercress, washed	2
1	onion, finely chopped	1
2 cups	chicken stock	500 mL
1 cup	skimmed milk	250 mL
2 tsp	grated lemon rind	10 mL
¼ tsp	freshly ground black pepper	1 mL
½ cup	plain low-fat yogurt	125 mL

1 Remove tough stems from watercress and chop leaves. Place leaves in a large saucepan with onion, stock, milk, lemon rind and pepper.

2 Simmer gently for 25 minutes, then purée mixture in a food processor or blender until smooth.

3 Stir in yogurt and chill. Serve garnished with watercress sprigs.

Serves 6

Chilled Avocado Soup with Salsa

1	large ripe avocado, halved, pitted and peeled	1
1 tbsp	freshly squeezed lime juice	15 mL
2 cups	chicken stock	500 mL
2 tbsp	chopped chives	30 mL
¾ cup	light cream	185 mL

SALSA

½	small onion, quartered	½
1	drained canned pimiento	1
1	garlic clove, halved	1
½	red chili pepper, seeded	½
2	fresh coriander sprigs	2
1 cup	chopped canned tomatoes	250 mL

1 Combine avocado, lime juice, chicken stock and chives in a blender or food processor. Process until smooth. Add cream and process for 30 seconds, then transfer to a soup tureen or serving bowl. Chill.

2 Meanwhile, make salsa. Roughly chop onion, pimiento, garlic, chili pepper and coriander in a blender or food processor. Add tomatoes and process briefly until combined.

3 Serve soup in chilled bowls, garnishing each portion with salsa.

Serves 4

Chicken Stock

You can use chicken trimmings such as wing tips and bones. Or you can use chicken parts (or a whole chicken cut into serving pieces) if you want the meat for another use.

3 lbs	chicken	1.5 kg
10 cups	water	2.5 L
3	sprigs parsley	3
1	onion, chopped	1
1	carrot, chopped	1
1	celery stalk, chopped	1
1	leek, trimmed and chopped	1
1	bay leaf	1
1/2 tsp	pepper	2 mL
1/4 tsp	dried thyme	1 mL
	salt to taste	

1. Place chicken in a large saucepan or stockpot with the water, chopped vegetables and seasonings. Bring to a boil, then skim off foam. Cook, covered, over low heat for 1 to 3 hours, or until chicken is tender.

2. Remove and reserve chicken. Strain liquid through a sieve, pressing to remove all possible liquid. Chill stock, then skim fat from surface. Stock can be frozen, or refrigerated for 2-3 days.

Makes 8-10 cups (2-2.5 L)

Basic Vegetable Stock

2	large unpeeled potatoes, quartered	2
2	large carrots, coarsely chopped	2
1	large onion, peeled and coarsely chopped	1
1	celery stalk, chopped	1
1	bay leaf	1
12	peppercorns	12
10 cups	water	2.5 L

1. Put all ingredients into a large saucepan or stockpot. Bring to a boil, then lower heat and simmer, covered, for about 1 hour. Strain and remove solids.

2. To make a sweeter stock, you can add a chopped apple or pear to the above ingredients, or include some parsnips, sweet potato or squash.

3. Garlic cloves and a small amount of tomato will produce a stronger-flavored stock. Add ginger and green onions for Asian flavor.

4. Avoid using the strongly flavored members of the cabbage family, including broccoli, cauliflower and turnips.

Makes 8 cups (2 L)

Soup Garnishes

A sprinkling of chopped fresh parsley is the universal soup garnish, but there are many more ways of enhancing the appearance of both hot and chilled soups.

Herb sprigs
Mint, chervil and coriander spring to mind, but there are alternatives. Try borage (including flowers and leaves) for chilled cucumber soups, and basil or marjoram for any soup that includes tomatoes. Dill is traditionally used for any fish soup.

Croûtons
Cubes of bread fried in oil or butter until golden and crisp. If you wish, flavor the oil with garlic. Croûtons are for robust soups like gazpacho.

Pastry decorations
Use puff pastry (store-bought is the most convenient) to make pastry crescents. Roll out the pastry thinly and cut out small circles using a small round cookie cutter or a liqueur glass. Move the cookie cutter half a circle to the side and cut through each circle to make a crescent and an oval shape. Bake the crescents on ungreased baking sheets at 400°F (200°C) for about 10 minutes, or until golden. (The oval pastry shapes can be rerolled, or sprinkled with grated cheese and baked to make cheese biscuits.)

Vegetable matchsticks and julienne
Vegetables such as carrots, parsnips or rutabaga make an attractive garnish for a clear soup such as a consommé when cut into thin sticks. Cook the vegetables briefly in boiling water, refresh them under cold water, and drain thoroughly before adding to the soup.

Cream swirl
A swirl design makes for a dramatic presentation of plain cream soups. Drizzle cream in a spiral pattern onto the soup, then drag a skewer or knife tip through the cream to make radiating lines. You can also pipe dollops of cream around the perimeter of the soup, and drag a skewer through the circles to make a pattern of heart shapes.

Sandwiches
and Snacks

The invention of the sandwich was clearly a boon for people on the go, making a quick meal that is even easy to pack and carry. And there is no doubt that a sandwich paired with a bowl of soup makes a satisfying, relaxed meal.

But sandwiches are also an appropriate choice for more elegant occasions. In this chapter, we have included some sophisticated sandwich ideas that are ideal for midday snacks or light evening entertaining, as well as some interesting variations on familiar family favorites. Use these recipes to spark your own imagination!

TOASTED ALLIGATORS

Toasted Alligators

1	loaf French bread, halved lengthwise	1
3 tbsp	butter	45 mL
5 oz	mortadella or salami, thinly sliced	150 g
2	tomatoes, sliced	2
1/4 lb	Jarlsberg or Cheddar cheese, thinly sliced	110 g
6	anchovy fillets	6
6	black olives, chopped, or stuffed olives, sliced	6
	fruit chutney	
	freshly ground black pepper	

♦ ♦ ♦

1. Toast bread, crust-side-up, under a preheated broiler until golden.

2. Spread untoasted surfaces with butter, then chutney. Cover bottom half of bread with mortadella or salami, tomatoes, and cheese, folding slices if too large. Decorate with anchovies and olives. Warm sandwiches in a hot oven, or broil until cheese is bubbly. Season with black pepper to taste.

3. Top loaf with remaining half and press down firmly. Cut diagonally into 3 or 4 lengths and serve.

Serves 3-4

French Bread Tartare

1	long loaf French bread	1
6 tbsp	butter, softened	90 mL
1	large garlic clove, crushed	1
3/4 lb	lean steak, finely chopped	350 g
1	egg, beaten	1
1 tsp	salt	5 mL
1/2 tsp	freshly ground black pepper	2 mL
6	green onions, finely chopped (include some green tops)	6
2 tbsp	finely chopped capers	30 mL
	dash Worcestershire sauce	

♦ ♦ ♦

1. Preheat oven to 400°F (200°C). Cut loaf in half lengthwise and scoop out centers. Combine butter and garlic and spread over insides of bread halves. Place loaf, cut-side-up, on a baking sheet and bake for 5 minutes or until golden.

2. Mix remaining ingredients together and correct seasoning. Fill bottom half of loaf with steak mixture and press top half back into place. Wrap tightly in foil and chill for 2 hours. Cut into thin slices and serve.

Serves 6

TIP: For this twist on the classic raw beef mixture, it is a good idea to chop or grind good-quality steak at home, since freshness is vitally important. If you must buy it from the butcher, ask him to grind it fresh.

Avocado and Bacon Sandwich

1	ripe avocado, halved and pitted	1
2	slices wholewheat or rye toast, buttered	2
5-6	small lettuce leaves	5-6
1	tomato, sliced	1
1 1/2 tbsp	vinaigrette dressing (optional)	25 mL
2	large bacon slices	2
	salt and freshly ground black pepper	

♦ ♦ ♦

1. Peel avocado and slice thickly. Place each slice of toast on a plate and arrange lettuce, tomato and avocado on top. Season to taste with salt and black pepper and a little vinaigrette, if desired.

2. Cut bacon strips in half and cook in a dry skillet over medium heat until browned. Tip bacon and some of the hot bacon drippings over sandwiches and serve immediately.

Serves 2

Mustardy Bratwurst Rolls

4	long soft bread rolls, slit lengthwise	4
6	green onions, finely chopped	6
3-4 tbsp	chopped mixed fresh herbs	45-60 mL
4	hot grilled bratwurst sausages	4
	Dijon mustard	
	salt and freshly ground black pepper	
	melted butter	

♦ ♦ ♦

1. Pull out some of the soft centers from each half roll. Brush insides with butter and sprinkle with green onions and herbs.

2. Split sausages lengthwise, and fill with mustard. Place a sausage in each hollowed roll, season to taste and press roll back together. Wrap in foil and refrigerate several hours.

3. Preheat oven to 350°F (180°C). Heat rolls, still in foil, for 20 minutes. Unwrap for last 2 minutes to crisp.

Serves 4

TIP: *If you do not have fresh mixed herbs, use chopped fresh parsley with 1 tsp (5 mL) dried mixed herbs.*

Roast Beef with Blue Cheese

4	5 inch (12 cm) lengths of French bread	4
1/4 lb	Blue cheese	110 g
1 cup	watercress sprigs	250 mL
1 lb	thinly sliced rare roast beef	450 g
4 tbsp	mayonnaise	60 mL
1 tbsp	drained, bottled horseradish	15 mL
	salt and freshly ground black pepper	

♦ ♦ ♦

1. Split bread sections horizontally leaving halves attached. Spread cut sides with Blue cheese, then top with watercress sprigs and beef slices.

2. In a bowl, combine mayonnaise and horseradish. Drizzle over beef. Season sandwiches with salt and black pepper to taste and close them, pressing firmly.

Serves 4

Herb-Spiked Vegetable Sandwich

1/2 cup	mayonnaise	125 mL
1 tsp	curry powder	5 mL
8	slices of country-style bread	8
2	firm tomatoes, sliced	2
1	English cucumber, peeled if desired and thinly sliced diagonally	1
1	red onion, thinly sliced	1
	fresh basil and mint leaves	
	salt and freshly ground black pepper	

♦ ♦ ♦

1. In a small bowl, combine mayonnaise and curry powder. Spread mixture on 1 side of each slice of bread.

2. Top half the bread slices with tomatoes, cucumber, onion and basil. Sprinkle with salt and black pepper to taste and add a layer of mint leaves. Top sandwiches with remaining bread slices. Press together firmly.

Serves 4

CLOCKWISE FROM LEFT: MUSTARDY BRATWURST ROLLS, ROAST BEEF WITH BLUE CHEESE, ZINGY CHICKEN CLUB (SEE P. 70), SMOKED GOUDA AND ROASTED PEPPER ROLLS, HERB-SPIKED VEGETABLE SANDWICH.

Smoked Gouda and Roasted Pepper Rolls

8	black olives, pitted	8
1 tbsp	lemon juice	15 mL
1/4 cup	olive oil	60 mL
1/2	garlic clove	1/2
4	4 inch (10 cm) lengths Italian bread, halved	4
1	large red bell pepper, roasted and quartered	1
1/2 lb	Smoked Gouda, thinly sliced	225 g
	cayenne pepper	
	fresh basil leaves	

1. In a blender or food processor, process olives, lemon juice, oil, garlic and cayenne pepper to taste until smooth. Brush cut sides of bread with this mixture.

2. Divide roasted pepper, cheese and basil between bread halves. Replace top halves and press sandwiches together firmly.

KITCHEN TIP: To roast pepper, pierce with a fork and char the skin until almost black and blistered over a gas flame, or under a preheated broiler, turning often, for 15 minutes. Place in a paper bag and let stand until cool enough to handle. Peel off skin and discard ribs and seeds.

Grilled Ham and Cheese

8	slices of French bread	8
4	slices ham	4
4	slices Swiss cheese	4
	butter	
	Dijon mustard	
	freshly ground black pepper	

◆ ◆ ◆

1 Spread bread generously with butter, then spread a little mustard on 4 slices and top with ham, cheese, black pepper to taste and remaining bread slices.

2 Press sandwiches together firmly and trim crust, if you like. Cut into two triangles or leave whole.

3 Melt a generous amount of butter in a skillet over medium heat. Add sandwiches and cook for 3-4 minutes on each side or until golden. Drain on paper towels and serve hot.

Variation

If you like, the sandwiches can be dipped into a mixture of 2 beaten eggs and 1/2 cup (125 mL) milk before frying.

Serves 4

Focaccia Heroes

1	garlic clove, crushed	1
2 tbsp	butter, softened	30 mL
1	large piece focaccia (enough for 4)	1
16	slices hot Italian salami or 4 slices ham	16
2	tomatoes, sliced	2
1	red onion, thinly sliced	1
1	red bell pepper, seeded and sliced	1
4	pinches fresh oregano	4
4	slices Jarlsberg cheese	4

♦ ♦ ♦

1. Mash garlic into softened butter until combined. Cut focaccia into 4 equal pieces. Slice each piece in half horizontally and brush with butter mixture. Divide remaining ingredients equally on half of focaccia pieces, ending with cheese.

2. Place layered focaccia along with the reserved buttered focaccia pieces under a preheated broiler until cheese is melted and bread is brown. Replace top halves and serve warm.

Serves 4

Zingy Chicken Club

4	slices lean bacon	4
2	boneless chicken breast fillets	2
12	thick slices white or brown bread	12
1/2 cup	mayonnaise	125 mL
8	lettuce leaves, rinsed and dried	8
8	thin slices tomato	8
8	thin slices red onion	8
	freshly ground black pepper	

♦ ♦ ♦

1. Place bacon in a small heavy skillet and cook until crisp. Drain on paper towels, reserving 1 tbsp (15 mL) fat in pan.

2. Add fillets to pan, season with pepper to taste and cook for 5-6 minutes on each side or until tender. Drain and set chicken aside to cool for 10 minutes, then cut into thin slices.

3. Toast bread. Spread mayonnaise on 1 side of 4 slices of toast and sprinkle with black pepper to taste. Add a lettuce leaf and 1 slice each of tomato, onion and bacon. Place another slice of toast on top and add another lettuce leaf and slice of onion, tomato and chicken. Finish with another slice of toast, and press together firmly. Cut sandwiches diagonally in half. If desired, secure with toothpicks topped with stuffed olives.

Serves 4

Dainty Open-Face Sandwiches

loaves of French bread
softened butter

SUGGESTED FILLINGS

smoked turkey slices with cranberry jelly
sliced roast beef with béarnaise sauce
sliced hard-boiled egg and caviar
peeled cooked giant shrimp and mango chutney
tomato, avocado and chopped fried bacon
smoked salmon with Camembert cheese and capers
sliced salami, cheese and pickles
ham and asparagus

GARNISHES

lettuce, olives, cherry tomatoes, lemon slices, watercress, basil, mild onion rings, fresh herbs (chives, basil, parsley, rosemary, dill)

♦ ♦ ♦

1. Slice French bread thinly. Lightly butter one side of each slice. Add any of the suggested toppings — or invent toppings of your own. Garnish as desired.

TIP: These sandwiches should be assembled just before serving. Have the bread buttered and covered, and prepare the ingredients ahead of time, placing them in covered containers in the refrigerator. Any type of bread may be used; the best are the firmer varieties such as rye and pumpernickel, which are easy to pick up and eat. Use sauces, herb butters or mayonnaise to ensure that the toppings adhere to the bread.

DAINTY OPEN-FACE SANDWICHES

Special Occasion Sandwiches

1/4 lb	smoked salmon	110 g
1/2 lb	cream cheese, softened	225 g
2	green onions, finely chopped	2
1/2	garlic clove, crushed	1/2
2 tbsp	chopped fresh parsley	30 mL
1 tbsp	chopped chives	15 mL
18	slices white sandwich bread	18

♦ ♦ ♦

1. Combine smoked salmon with half the cream cheese in a blender or food processor. Purée until smooth. Scrape into a bowl.

2. Place remaining cream cheese in clean food processor or blender. Add green onions, garlic, parsley and chives. Process until mixture is smooth. Transfer to a second bowl. Cover both bowls and refrigerate for 2 hours or until firm.

3. Cut off crusts from bread slices. Spread six slices with smoked salmon mixture and six slices with herb mixture. Assemble triple decker sandwiches by placing one herb bread slice on top of each smoked salmon bread slice, adding a plain bread slice on top.

4. Cut each sandwich into four triangles. Serve immediately or refrigerate, covered with a damp cloth, for up to 4 hours.

Makes 24 triangles

Scrambled Egg and Smoked Salmon Sandwiches

4 tbsp	butter, plus extra for spreading	60 mL
8	eggs	8
½ cup	whipping cream	125 mL
1 tbsp	chopped chives	15 mL
4	slices bread	4
4	slices smoked salmon	4

1. Melt butter in a medium saucepan over medium heat. Using a fork, mix eggs, cream and chives in a bowl until well combined. Pour mixture into saucepan and cook for 2-3 minutes, stirring occasionally, or until eggs are lightly scrambled.

2. Butter bread, lay a slice of smoked salmon on each slice, and top with scrambled eggs. Serve immediately.

Makes 4

Grilled Mozzarella and Prosciutto Sandwiches

½ lb	mozzarella, shredded	225 g
½ cup	Ricotta cheese	125 mL
¼ lb	prosciutto, cut into thin strips	110 g
1	tomato, seeded, and chopped	1
1	egg, beaten	1
12	slices bread	12
2 tbsp	unsalted butter	30 mL
2 tbsp	olive oil	30 mL
	salt and freshly ground black pepper	

1. Combine mozzarella, ricotta, prosciutto, tomato and egg in a bowl. Mix well. Season to taste with salt and freshly ground pepper.

2. Spread mixture onto 6 bread slices, and top with remaining bread.

3. Heat butter and oil in a large skillet over medium heat. Add sandwiches in batches, and fry until golden and cheese has melted, about 2 minutes each side. Serve hot.

Makes 6

Open-Face Smoked Turkey and Stilton Sandwiches

2 tbsp	Dijon mustard	30 mL
12	thick slices French bread, buttered	12
12	slices smoked turkey	12
½ lb	Stilton cheese	225 g
	watercress sprigs for garnish	

♦ ♦ ♦

1 Spread mustard on each slice of buttered bread and top with slice of turkey and crumbled Stilton. Garnish each slice with a watercress sprig.

Serves 4

Toasted Smoked Ham and Gruyère with Fried Onion

3 tbsp	unsalted butter, softened	45 mL
1	large Spanish onion, thinly sliced	1
8	thin slices crusty white bread	8
8	thin slices Gruyère cheese	8
8	slices smoked ham	8
	freshly ground black pepper	

♦ ♦ ♦

1. Melt 1 tbsp (15 mL) of butter in a heavy-based, nonstick skillet. Add onion and sauté until softened and golden, about 5 minutes. Set aside.

2. Spread remaining butter on bread, one side only. Place 4 slices, buttered side down, on a flat surface. Top each with 1 slice of cheese and 2 slices of ham.

3. Place fried onion on top of ham, and season with freshly ground pepper. Top with remaining cheese and place remaining slices of bread on top, buttered side up.

4. Cook sandwiches under a preheated broiler until cheese has melted and sandwiches are golden, about 6 minutes, turning once. Serve immediately.

Serves 4

Roasted Red Pepper and Ricotta Sandwiches

2	roasted red peppers, halved (see Tip page 67)	2
1 cup	Ricotta cheese	250 mL
2/3 cup	grated Parmesan cheese	165 mL
1 tbsp	chopped chives	15 mL
4	thick slices wholewheat bread	4
1	red onion, thinly sliced	1
	fresh parsley for garnish	

♦ ♦ ♦

1. In a small bowl, combine Ricotta cheese, Parmesan cheese and chives, mix well.

2. Spread Ricotta cheese mixture on each slice of bread, top with a roasted pepper half and onion rings, and garnish with parsley sprigs.

Serves 4

Roasted Red Pepper and Ricotta Sandwiches, Chicken and avocado Sandwiches

Chicken and Avocado Sandwiches

4	slices bread	4
2 oz	cream cheese, softened	60 g
4 tbsp	mayonnaise	60 mL
6 oz	sliced cooked chicken	180 g
4	slices aged Cheddar cheese	4
1	avocado, peeled, pitted and sliced	1
1 tbsp	chopped chives	15 mL

♦ ◆ ♦

1. On each slice of bread spread cream cheese, then mayonnaise. Top with chicken and slice of cheese and broil until cheese has melted.

2. Top with avocado and sprinkle with chives. Serve at once.

Serves 4

Chicken Tacos

8	taco shells	8
1 tbsp	oil	15 mL
½	onion, finely chopped	½
4	tomatoes, chopped	4
1 tbsp	chopped fresh parsley	15 mL
¾ lb	cooked chicken, chopped	350 g
1 cup	Cheddar cheese, grated	250 mL

◆ ◆

1. Preheat oven to 325°F (160°C). Heat taco shells on a large baking sheet in oven for 12 minutes.

2. Meanwhile fry onion in oil in a medium saucepan until soft. Add tomatoes and parsley and cook over medium heat for 10 minutes. Stir in chicken.

3. Fill each taco shell with chicken and tomato mixture, then top with grated cheese. Serve immediately.

Serves 4

TIP: *This is a very mild taco recipe. You may want to serve bottled taco sauce or hot pepper sauce on the side. Slices of peeled avocado also make a nice addition.*

Mini Prosciutto Pizzas

2	crusty bread rolls or English muffins, cut in half	2
3 tbsp	tomato paste	45 mL
8	small slices prosciutto	8
4	slices Mozzarella cheese	4
2 tbsp	finely chopped red bell pepper	30 mL
2 tbsp	chopped fresh parsley	30 mL

◆ ◆ ◆

1 Preheat oven to 350°F (180°C). Toast rolls or English muffins lightly. Spread tomato paste on each half roll. Top with two slices of prosciutto, then add cheese. Combine red pepper and parsley in a small bowl and sprinkle a quarter of mixture over each roll.

2 Arrange rolls on a baking sheet. Bake for 10 minutes or until cheese has melted. Serve at once.

Serves 2

Variations

Pita pizzas: Slit small pita breads in half through the middle. Arrange on baking sheets with the soft bread on top. Top as suggested above or with thinly sliced tomatoes, onions and crisp fried bacon. Omit the mozzarella; sprinkle with grated Cheddar cheese instead. Bake as suggested above.

Ham and Cheddar Flatbread Pizza

2	rounds of flatbread or naan bread	2
2 tbsp	tomato paste	30 mL
1/4 lb	cooked ham, chopped	110 g
1 cup	Cheddar cheese, grated	250 mL
1 tbsp	chopped fresh parsley	15 mL

♦ ♦ ♦

1. Preheat oven to 350°F (180°C). Spread tomato paste thinly on each flatbread round. Sprinkle ham, cheese and parsley on top.

2. Bake for 15 minutes. Serve in slices.

Makes 8 slices

Variations

Add any of the following, or a combination: crumbled fried bacon, lightly cooked sliced mushrooms, sliced pepperoni sausage, drained canned tuna flakes, or red, green or yellow pepper strips lightly fried in oil. Fresh herbs add an elegant note.

MEASURING MADE EASY

LENGTH

Inches	Centimeters	Inches	Centimeters
1/4	0.5 (5 mm)	7	18
1/2	1	8	20
3/4	2	9	23
1	2.5	10	25
1 1/2	4	12	30
2	5	14	35
2 1/2	6	16	40
3	7.5	18	45
4	10	20	50
6	15		

NB: 1 cm = 10 mm

METRIC SPOON SIZES

1/4 teaspoon	=	1 mL
1/2 teaspoon	=	2 mL
1 teaspoon	=	5 mL
1 tablespoon	=	15 mL

LIQUIDS

1/8 cup	30 mL
1/4 cup	60 mL
1/3 cup	85 mL
1/2 cup	125 mL
2/3 cup	165 mL
3/4 cup	185 mL
1 cup	250 mL
1 1/4 cups	310 mL
1 1/3 cups	330 mL
1 1/2 cups	375 mL
1 3/4 cups	440 mL
2 cups	500 mL
2 1/4 cups	560 mL
2 1/3 cups	585 mL
2 1/2 cups	625 mL
2 3/4 cups	685 mL
3 cups	750 mL
4 cups	1 L
5 cups	1.2 L
6 cups	1.5 L

WEIGHTS

1/8 lb	60 g
1/4 lb	110 g
1/3 lb	150 g
1/2 lb	225 g
2/3 lb	300 g
3/4 lb	350 g
1 lb	450 g
1 1/4 lbs	560 g
1 1/3 lbs	600 g
1 1/2 lbs	675 g
1 3/4 lbs	800 g
2 lbs	1 kg
3 lbs	1.5 kg

Index

Artichoke and Shrimp Bisque	22
Avocado and Bacon Sandwich	65
Avocado Summer Soup	6
Basic Vegetable Stock	60
Basil and Almond Soup	31
Beggar's Soup	13
Borscht	52
Carrot Soup with Coriander	28
Chestnut Soup	38
Chicken and Avocado Sandwiches	75
Chicken Stock	60
Chicken Tacos	76
Chilled Apple and Fennel Soup	54
Chilled Avocado Soup with Salsa	59
Chilled Butternut Soup	53
Chilled Coriander and Yogurt Soup	8
Chilled Indian Cucumber Soup	56
Chilled Melon and Cucumber Soup	6
Chilled Roasted Red Pepper Soup	34
Chilled Spinach Soup with Sour Cream	6
Chilled Tomato and Avocado Soup	52
Chilled Watercress and Lemon Soup	58
Chunky Meat and Chickpea Soup	18
Classic Leek and Potato Soup	31
Cream of Corn and Red Pepper Soup	8
Cream of Summer Squash Soup	7
Creamy Mushroom Soup	44
Curried Lamb Soup with Split Peas	19
Dainty Open-Face Sandwiches	70
Dilled Carrot and Sweet Potato Soup	45
Easy French Onion Soup	22
Fennel Soup	38
Focaccia Heroes	69
French Bread Tartare	64
Fruity Spinach Soup	48
Garlic Soup	43
Gazpacho	56
Green Minestrone	41
Grilled Ham and Cheese	68
Grilled Mozzarella and Prosciutto Sandwiches	72
Ham and Cheddar Flatbread Pizza	78
Hearty Bean and Vegetable Soup	46
Hearty Beef and Brussels Sprout Soup	21
Herb-Spiked Vegetable Sandwich	66
Italian Fettuccine Consommé	12
Leek Soup with Thyme	40
Macaroni and Vegetable Soup	11
Mediterranean Vegetable and Pasta Soup	49
Minestrone with Pesto	32
Mini Prosciutto Pizzas	77
Miso Soup	46
Mixed Vegetable Soup	29
Mulligatawny Soup	35
Mushroom and Barley Soup	39
Mushroom Vegetable Soup	26
Mustardy Bratwurst Rolls	66
Noodle Soup with Basil and Meatballs	16
Old-Fashioned Pumpkin Soup	43
Open-Face Smoked Turkey and Stilton Sandwiches	73
Pea and Ham Soup	16
Pork Ball and Broccoli Soup	17
Potato Soup with Croûtons	35
Roast Beef with Blue Cheese	66
Roasted Red Pepper and Ricotta Sandwiches	74
Scrambled Egg and Smoked Salmon Sandwiches	72
Smoked Gouda and Roasted Pepper Rolls	67
Smoked Salmon Soup	24
Soup Garnishes	61
Special Occasion Sandwiches	71
Spinach Soup with Sausage Meatballs	20
Toasted Alligators	64
Toasted Smoked Ham and Gruyère with Fried Onion	74
Tomato and Shellfish Soup	25
Tomato Dill Soup	55
Tuscan Bean Soup	26
Watercress Soup with Orange	8
Yogurt Soup	10
Zingy Chicken Club	70